# It is not perfect

by
**Jacqueline Hall**

Grosvenor House
Publishing Limited

This book is published by
Grosvenor House Publishing Ltd
Link House
140 The Broadway, Tolworth, Surrey, KT6 7HT.
www.grosvenorhousepublishing.co.uk

A CIP record for this book
is available from the British Library

Paperback ISBN 978-1-83615-193-7
eBook ISBN 978-1-83615-194-4

To B

# Contents

# Kilbrannan Sound

## for Jo

We changed the shore forever
For a short time

Throwing the round rocks
Into the sea
Obsessed
Hurling for the sound of suck
What were we doing?
Thinking of you
Not thinking
Delighting in those heavy eggs
Heavier and heavier
And round

# Kissing

I don't think of it
Don't expect it
Except sometimes at night
In the half light of pillow,
Arm and curtain

I am living with a no
I hold a membrane of not thinking,
Wanting, touching
An impalpable wall
Between nothing and not nothing

# Full Moon in Leeds 2015, Remembering Ann

Full moon in Leeds tonight revealed in milky cloud,
    above the Corn Exchange
Thinking of writing what I wanted to tell you
My mother's pleasure at the silhouette of leafless trees
Not knowing which she loved most, the winter or the
    summer forms
Which I feel now, feeling shapes I hadn't seen before

Along the bottom of the woods, Dog's Mercury,
    the first plant to appear in spring,
Tiny florets, then up the hill, tents of thin branches
    in the Beechwoods
Encampments made by children, further
Up the ridge, the view appears, we start to reach
    the tops of trees
Resting against the trunk, mist stretches out above the
    canopies of green

Then climbing higher, steeper now, past March cold
The milkwort appears - pure joy - on the chalky turf
Kites wheel, young kites mew, many circle
Some glide so near their shaggy headdress wings are clear
Brown – white – black – visible, their feathers are
    like quills

Then later the gorgeous dropwort, like lace of bridal veils
And the call of the willow warbler, almost as delirious
As the cuckoo - 'I am here, I am here…
        please come or let me come to you
I have journeyed to these bushes to sing my heart out,
Compelled to mate and make this glorious sound'

You made me hear it, a town child, like the feral
        smell of fox
Which was noticed but not known
And what of reading? Was it different or the same
This reading that I learnt from you? Inseparable
I don't feel now I could learn one without the other
Like knowing the tiny skylark was not crying out in panic
Wanting to be rescued but was singing as it should be,
Hovering in the air above its nest

Common orchids in the chalk path past the earth works
Clumps of violets along the verge of the bottom track
Foundations of the house above the stockyard
That only you could really see, where we would rest
And once watched hares boxing in the snowy field
Always things to watch. Another time
A thundering hare brushed past our legs, set up by Jones
Swerving so near I felt the moved air as it braked
        and turned

In the autumn walking out quietly past the paddock,
At dusk, the shadows on a ridge and furrow field
I hadn't seen before, the house and chestnut tree behind,
'Always at this time' you said as you looked up
And I followed your head and eyes, as I learnt to do
To sweeping flocks of birds, I hadn't noticed

Too high to identify,
Lone squawks and distant calls
Familiar and unfamiliar, black rivers in the sky
Transit of biblical proportion,
Flooding - dissolving and reforming, wave after wave
Mysterious, purposeful migration
And you, who usually knew all
Didn't know what birds they were
Or where they were going to
As we stood and watched in silence
My heart full

# Dutch Elm, Ladywell Fields
## for Maggie Fagan

It seemed the world would not renew
But in a nearby field I discovered,
Alongside catkins and daffodils and gorse in bloom,

A magnificent Dutch Elm which grew
By the side of the Ravensbourne river.
The only one in London to survive, so

The sign said. The water cleaving the two
Banks was sharp as polished silver,
A strip of dazzling light. Geese flew

In ribbon V formation against the blue
Of cloudless sky, the weather
Perfect for their journey of migration to

Their other home, I wish I knew -
North or South, I could not remember.
Transported by their flight and the tree so

Unexpectedly come through
When I thought all had gone forever,
The dark days lifted, and you
Recovered in the towering elm and life anew

# Walk to Stelling Wood, October 2020

'Take abundance from abundance
And abundance remains'
(Isha Upanishad)


We climbed and reached the path
Running parallel, so near to the route we knew
But high up on the edge of the valley
Muddy, narrow, ancient,
Ghostly stems of umbellifers to the meadow on our side
Buzzards mewed as we walked along
Glided low above us
Hawthorn bushes, variously sporting berries
One completely covered in red
Was it the pylon overhead?
My dear friend wondered.

Then down the Holloway
Funneled like a wave in leaf
Honey fungus to the side

Walking, walking, heavy weights on backs and shoulders
Sitting down, then moving on
Round a corner exquisite scent
A small orchard of apple trees
Tentatively tracing, losing, delicate and faint perfume

Suddenly face to face with bees
And flowers and leaves in clusters, dense and dry
And pointed and not known
Multiply alive. So many different kinds
White tail, smaller, honey bees
And my large face, a bit afraid but heady too
So close to source
(Of Chilean Myrtle, I later found)

Jill then said a bumble bee will raise its hand
To warn not to come so near and keep a distance
A helpful and universal gesture, it seems, if you know
Or are told or really look to see what is being said
Which only few do
(I am pleased I know those who do – Jill,
My sister too, who guide my eyes and ears)

Then walking into Garlinge Green
Cyclamen all along the track
First the Black and then the White cottage
One lived in and one empty on the corner,
    garden running riot,
Pulling at my heart.
I moved into both with my eyes as I passed
And many others,
Lived the other side

Then into ancient Petham in the dip
And up the hill to Duck Pit Lane,
The last part of our journey.
A field rising sharply to the left
And on the right, gradual incline, farms and horses
Sweet Chestnut, Rowan, Spindle, Hazel

The God Cake at Ansdore
Where we rested and had a late lunch of the little food
     we'd taken
Looking up at the trees and wires, tarmac
Held up by roots
Glorious, hidden, quiet track
Secret valley

Finally turning to the steep slope and its wooded crest
Jill talking of the alps
Huge effort to mount the vertical stile, pulled back
     by gravity
Then over the peak to
Devastation
An orchard gone, razed to straggly stumps and
     a carpet of ashy lime
Sad walk across the fields
Which had been ripe and red, criss-crossed with
     intriguing scat
Past the farm and along the track
The edge of the wood in sight now
Arrested by two dead foxes laying side by side,
     no mark on them
Burnished coats and brush
Perfect, as if asleep.
More questions and a sense of shock and sadness

A young man steps out from behind the trees
And onto the path, deciding to be seen
Although my friend had spotted him
Dressed in neat country clothes and hat
Seems decent,
Says he didn't kill them when we ask but

Is shooting pigeons at the farmers' request
Jill tells him it's her wood

Finally, we turn aside from the Wayleave and are in at last
Dark clouds gathering we made our camp
Then moved it, clumsy now with tiredness,
Under the shelter when it rained

Supper of sardine and egg
A small fierce fire
Then into our bivvy bags, top to toe,
And the night long effort to keep warm

Talking at first, then drifting off
Thrilled and happy to be outside, in the wood
The owls hooting and calling

Meditating, I thought,
Diamonds of light along my body
Shining brightly
In the blackness
At that moment Jill shouted
'Oi' 'Oi'
I came to
An instant later thunder and vibration of heavy steps
    just by my ear
A deer surely!

No! A badger come to explore
Its face a foot or so away from Jill's
When she awoke, looming in the shadows
Both transfixed

Attracted by the smell of our supper, no doubt,
And these funny long creatures on its patch
We lay awake
Our hearts full of excitement and the propinquity
Of the encounter

Later reluctantly getting out of the bag
To answer nature
First surprised by the sailing moon
In the now cloudless sky
And then the stars, glinting like sharp diamonds in the gaps
    between the trees
Vivid crystals of light

Later Jill said she saw
The night sky moving
In the space framed by the branches, like a grid
Incrementally perceptible
Vastness slowly turning
In the liquid of her eyes.

At last warmth in my back
The brief grey of dawn and then the full brightness of
    morning
A deep, late sleep!

Breakfast – pot noodle, sausage, chocolate
Dousing the fire and stashing our back packs to collect later
We began the walk back
Lighter, unencumbered

Descending the high wood, sharp eyed,
Jill found a young badger skull
Thrown up amongst the chalk of the soft burrows,
Its snout chewed off

Later, retracing the steps down Duck Pit Lane,
Jill spied a Death Coachman's beetle
Small at first but large in character, as details grew
Its jet black tail poised like a scorpion,
Two enormous pincers on each side
Sinister and Gothic,
Dwarfing the road.

Further, we watched a swirling flock of birds in the corner
   of a field
I heard, amongst the cries, distinctive, bubbling rill of
   skylark
But never seen them grouped before,
I doubted what I knew
Jill said she thought them meadow pipits and
Both of these, it seems, were true.
Later we learnt skylarks will join with other birds
In Autumn, foraging in crop stubble and fallow ground for
   weed seed and grain
Not only singular, as I believed,
But sociable, beyond themselves
(So much more to notice, read and know)

Finally, the home straight
Following on the path took us, virtually, to Jill's door.
In the afternoon light along Cockering road,
Either side our native hedgerow
Spindle, Rosehips, Rowans,
Wild Service, Hazel, Oak,
Red, green, gold, yellow
All the colours in between, more
Hawthorn, Beech and Maple
And the Guelder Rose

# Fox before the Class

The first class in person since Covid
Anticipation......A few minutes walk
And then
As I step through my door
A large fox on my front lawn

Surprise at such closeness!
I see his body in rare detail
The slender sharp shape of his nose and long back
But strong!

He spans the grass.
He looks at me but doesn't move
We know each other

I barely breathe to keep him there
Stock still
I want my class
But want him in my garden more

I say hello and click my teeth
He stands on
Looks away, unharried
Claims his ground

Moments of strange peace and wonder
Under the tree
Although my heart is racing, a little scared
He is so familiar with me
Sounds of a couple in the road
Disturb him
I watch them pass the gate, unaware
And he is gone

I look for him
But his large form
Has vanished into air

Spellbound, I arrive at my class
Forget and then remember
When, at the end,
Eyes closed and guided,
He surprises
And fills my sight again

September 2020

# New Cat

The curtain opened
To the first leaves turning
On the shimmering Black Poplar tree

Later, in the garden
Under the bushes where the fox likes to lie
Was a new cat

Face dappled by the shadows there
It yawned
I asked if it was tired

Settling on the bench
I looked out at the garden, in the morning light
Alone but not

The cat got up
Walked slowly towards me, shyly
Wanting contact

Through the open door
It leapt up on the counter
Its seeking head

Finding my stroking hand
Another cat come to stay
Or passing

Either way is fine

# My cat's mouth

She yawns, I see the perfect cavern of her mouth
Her ruddy tongue an elongated slide
Curved, rough and dainty

Either side her pointed, fork-like teeth
Thin ivory moons, that would be terrifying
If not so small and for the row of baby teeth between

Her soft pink, opalescent ears, diaphanous.
The delicate intensity of her rhythmic, dipping face
Drinking so thirsty and absorbed

I stop in my tracks, arrested.
Water in her new glass bowl - her vital need –
I see her separate self for the first time.

Later I look at my hands cupping
Her light head. They are my mother's hands

# New Year's Day walk in
# Larkey Valley Wood

Up Strangers Lane to Cockering Road
Back up the track we took before
A ley line in my soul, it seems,
It pulls with such a heartfelt draw

Some way along we spy a wood
A turn my friend says she has noticed
On previous treks but not explored
The path leads straight ahead

A short way in we see a sign of walks
Of different lengths - we won't go far today
But further pleasure lodges in my chest
Of anticipated discovery

Neglected birch coppice on our right
Then thriving chestnut coppice with young maple -
So fortunate to be informed of what we pass -
And then a clearing with woodpiles

And barriers of poles (to keep out deer?)
A medieval camp, it seems, with wooden throne
The dogs appear spellbound in this place,
We make a note to come back and commune

Retracing steps, a clump of light green leaves
My friend decides, after a pause, is Buddleia
Another path strikes off into the wood - this
Walk a preparation for more reconnoiter

Back on the lane, we study more green growth
Then straightening up I see a line of disparate trees
On the hill's crest - small, misty and forlorn -
Nothing yet everything, to me, of country

Winter, in that damp light, of separate life
That stands and leans against each other's shapes,
Against the wind, throughout all weathers,
Imprinted black and white and grey

Always but barely there on this short day
Then slowly turning back to the path below
We note the ash keys hanging up on high and
Hazel catkins in the hedge before we head for home

# Deep time in Norfolk

Indomitable the spirit of this woman
Eloquent, she used this for her neighbour
Older, driven, bowed
But not bowed,
By her bones

Cleavers, carpets of mauve red
Dead nettles
Cow parsley coming,
Daisies, unfamiliar,
Huge chamomile, perhaps
Fresh, shining flowers
In sporadic clumps

Dents de lion (the dandelion leaf explained)
Forget me nots,
Lords and ladies, violets

Sycamore saplings, Rooks
Calling, calling, cawing
Circling, cacophony
A colony of nests
In trees. I'm told
A rook alone is a crow and
A crow with others is a rook

Cotman field of sweeping tan
Behind the wood
The pack of dogs and cats
Swirl in a cloud
Around the girl
Chickens pecking on the path
Green black Ayam Cemanis and
Cream Legbars
Part of the magic clan

The neighbours' little baby four weeks old
Come with her parents in a sling
Sleeping on her mother's chest
Perfect head and body curved into cloth
So round, she still looked held inside
Her newness and calm beauty makes our day

In between I read about
The first geologists and Siccar Point,
Sentences indented with the weight
Of atoms, realisation
So recent of the age of earth,
Deep time,
It's too much to take in
I move between the wood and words

A mouse nest shown beneath
A metal tank we moved
A pile of small dry leaves,
Supple and soft,
Above a hollow with grey pellets,
Tell-tale, in its bed
Another revelation which, from now
I'll look for and may recognise and know

At night the brightest moon I've ever seen
It woke me, shining through the window
Of our cabin room, not full
But then outside it hurt my eyes to look
(Another first)
Big stars, like discs of rising dough
Owls hooting
Muntjac barking, barking
Not like a deer but like a dog, alone,
Quite near, with sharp teeth too
Best kept at bay

Just two days in the wood but
More to write and learn
With friends and friends of friends
Of words to use and tools
And where and how to look
At other lives and life

Than months at home

2021

# The Front Spine
## Claridge House, for Bernadette

I saw and felt my inner spine
For the first time today
A beautiful wave of bone
The neck beginning beneath the shoulder blades
The occiput a final upward curve, through which
The neural pathway flows
And then reposes

I saw inside to where the organs are enfolded
The cases of the pleura for the lungs
The pericardium for the heart
The lymph juice liquid and the blood
That circulates and swells and calms
And keeps the balance in our frame
Unseen but like the sea and spine, in waves
I heard it speak when lying down
We rocked our body with our heels
Its tingling resonance and heat
In myriad membranes when we stalled

''''''''''''''

The space inside the chest
Now visible with inward eye
Beyond all words its making

The interconnectedness of cells
The weightlessness of suspension, top to tail
The warmth like sand extending at the heels
The feeling of extension from the arms
The complete comfort of the back,
Each vertebra, it felt at rest
The profound knowledge of the hands
The unique envelope of the skin
Wherein every motion, even most minute
Contracts and expands
Across a range of unknown sensitivity
Until it lands and finds a level in stillness

The incalculable miracle of the breath
Surrounded by the trees
Who hold their arms around us
Within without
To take our breath
To take our breath
To take our breath

# On reading Claire Keegan's 'The Forester's Daughter'

'Art is a lie which reveals the truth'
– Picasso

This art that is everything and nothing
The distillation of all disappointment
Missed chances, hope
Wonder, betrayal, loyalty and
Love

Ordinary and extraordinary,
Restrained, hidden
Then announced
Beyond subtlety it is the
Closeness of being offered help
And beyond that of
Needing and accepting it
All disguises and defences gone

It is the love of one species
For another
Of hair and fur and warmth
Of dependency and independence
Of giving up
And starting again

It is not comparison
But connection beneath
Difference

Underground
What we don't see
The web beneath our feet
Mycelium in every cell

Homesickness and forgiveness,
Which is a way of finding home
Grace that comes unbidden
After the heavy toil of hurt

# Not saying goodbye

I didn't say goodbye
John closed the door
As I began to climb the steps
Leaving you to sleep

All the time
I'd been worrying about
What I'd say to you
See you later is what I decided
The intention to come back,
But, also, what I believed,
That we would see each other again
We'd be in the wood again
With the dogs and cats and friends
And fire and tools
And the rooks
Rising above us from their nests
And landing
Constant motion, calling
One becomes deaf to
You smiling, striding, sailing
Like a ship ahead,
Irrepressibly commanding,
Keen pleasure, joy and purpose

Not to Maggie either
I thought I'd see again
But as she looked up into
My eyes,
One eye light blue
Our last deep look
And smiling too
I told her I was there and that
Her loved ones would be back
And instead of saying goodbye that night,
Rinsed with sad dread
I watched her husband's friend
Say goodbye with such gentleness
It stayed with me all these years
Like my goodbye unsaid

No words can match that look
Which wasn't a goodbye

Steadfast helpmeets
Hold the rest
The blessed sleep of peace

# Colney Woodland, Norfolk

The room with trees surrounding
Tall, an infinite recession
Souls rising, risen looking in
The wooden jetty going out to
Footpaths and a woodland sea

Emily above,
The love and grief and awe
In that round house
Her shining, blazing, lovely self

Force of nature, forceful, fearless, 'not afraid'
Deep booming voice
Heart breaking, gorgeous smile
Her whole face blinking in

Tears, tears, tears and trees
Too much and not enough
Her poise and eloquent beauty
Angular, applying a blade or screw
With consummate precision

Turning up just in time in her
Overlarge white shirt
That is what perfection looks like
Emily

At night, again, back in the cabin
A star woke me so bright I could not look
Just like the first time I was here
I opened my eyes and tried to find it
At the corner of the panes,
Dark trees outside

No star appeared.
Again, I turned and tried to sleep
And there it was
Too bright to look at
Glinting large crystals, fiery white
Like blades
Eyes open fully, searching the squares
The star is nowhere to be seen

In the morning I told Jill
She wondered, quite naturally, if I'd thought that it was you
And I said, with some conviction, that I had

Where are you? You are everywhere
But most close to your home and John
And to your mother, Imerlin, in those trees
And Adam, your neighbours' little boy nearby
Guiding, leading, keeping an eye on him
Until his parents come
With your fierce loving heart and soul

Those tall trees, rising and shining
Illuminated with light
As we waited and gazed, cold and exhausted,
Amazed at the unexpected view
Suspended, only for a time,
Until we also join the trees
And look back in

# Light of the near full moon:
# Isle of Wight

Above the hedge the moon surprised us
It shone with preternatural brightness
As if its radiance flared directly
From itself, in molten silver fire,
Not as a mirror of the sun obscured

In truth, I forgot how the light came
To be reflected and felt half deranged
As I bathed in and gazed
At the Heavenly Body,
Pulling my blood upward
With love and longing
Like the sea

# Milky Way, Pissos

After an absence of three years
Due to the pandemic
I walk out with Fabrice
Into the garden at night
The sky so black and dense with stars,
Blazing, singing out their light
I reel in awe

After a while my eyes adjust
To the milky stain
Above a tree
Solidity of light
Deep space beyond
Darker than ink

Ordinary nocturnal sight
But, to me, a revelation
Now absent from most skies
Drained half with light
In London I count eleven stars
Above my house,
Straining to count so many
Here one hundred easily
Eleven hundred more
And Jupiter, I later learn,
The brightest body in the sky, by far,
Shining behind me
When I turn

Fabrice informs me the next day
We see the Milky Way on its side,
Like a coin,
Not looking at its face
Hence the unique glow and depth
Of its strange shape

Oblique wedge of pearly light
Like Holbein's anamorphic skull
Dwarfing the ambassadors
Seen hanging from below

Detached image of our inner world
Its heart and centre,
As we look back towards it
From our limb
Itself one tiny island
In an ocean of immensity

To see this clearly, rarely, here
When it is always there
Above me but obscured

Ever-renewed mystery
Of our infinitesimal place
From the lawn, on the earth, in the stars,
The width of our seeing
So vast and small
In the field of night

September 2022

# It is not perfect

It is not perfect
We think we fall in love with one person
But they are many
We think the same of ourselves
But neither are we one
But a composite inside
Some calm, some clutching
Some full of joy, some sad
Held together only by the organ
Of our skin

At least, sometimes, if fortunate,
We can reflect,
Our saving grace,
Stop and step back
Learn more
About the serious contact
Our love seeks
But can't assume

And if, more fortunate still,
We are allowed,
We step back in

# Toad under the Quince tree

In amongst the bushes
Under the Quince tree
I heard a squeak
I was cutting fruit from high branches
With an unruly telescopic pruner
And parting the undergrowth roughly
To look for what had fallen

The sound was high pitched -
Not known -
I felt afraid but
Had to keep on looking
It was a deep mystery -
Was it a snake
Or another small monster
That would bite or poison me?

I had to know
What was this creature?
It might be a fox cub,
Though very small,
Or a mouse or shrew, a mole
Or hedgehog

I moved the leaves gingerly
But with intense curiosity - and then
I saw a shiny, wet looking toad,
Flat and motionless

Light green, perfectly camouflaged
Or very nearly

It looked a little like a squashed fruit
And I hoped profoundly
A quince had not dropped
On its back

I let the leaves cover it again
Then looked a second and a third time
Not quite believing what I saw
And wishing to record it
With my phone
It started to move
Burrowing slowly
Into denser vegetation
And I let the shrubbery close over
Not wanting to disturb it further

It was so primeval
The wetness of the leaves and soil
The oozy moistness of its skin
A kind of glitter
Like the most earthly, earthy jewel

We have always had
Toads in this garden
It's just they have been
Largely hiding since my Mum
Has not been here

One last year in a flower pot
And now this beauty

In the undisturbed corner
Beneath the Quince tree
Where my mother's ashes lie

I knew she would be pleased,
Perhaps had arranged for me
To find this toad
And hear it speak
When I had never known
They had a voice before -
Perhaps surprised by my activity,
Impinged by hand or tool,
Or simply warning me of its presence
In the still, wild earth
To leave in peace
Under the Quince
And Black Poplar tree

# About the Author

Jacqueline Hall was born in London and grew up in Blackheath. She studied English Literature at St Hugh's College, Oxford University, before later training to be an NHS Child and Adolescent Psychotherapist at the Tavistock Clinic. She continued to work there as a clinician and trainer for the remainder of her career, as well as in multi-agency and fostering and adoption services in Camden and Kent. She is now retired and divides her time between her homes in South London and Walmer, on the Kent coast.